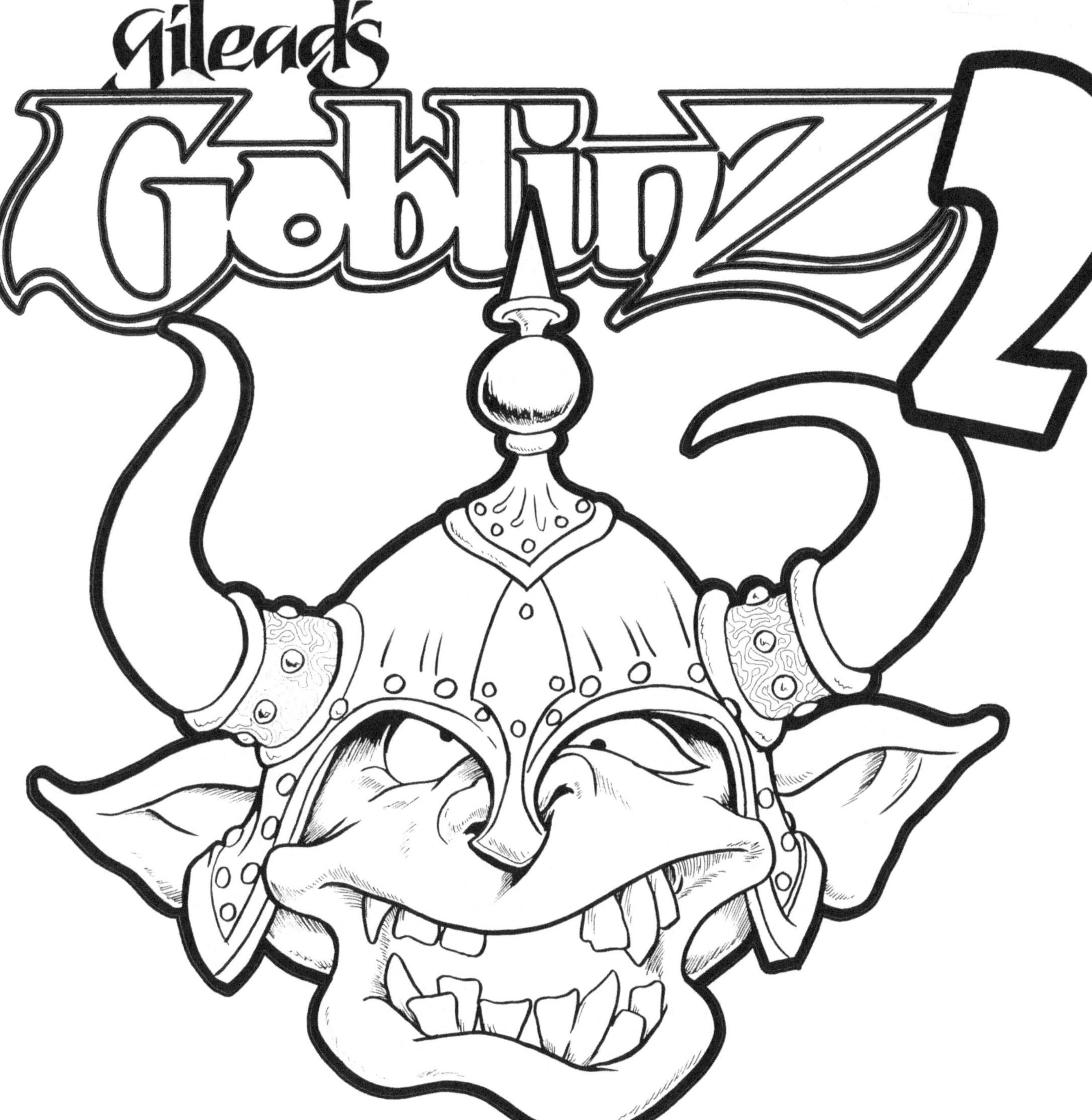

Made in the U.S.A.

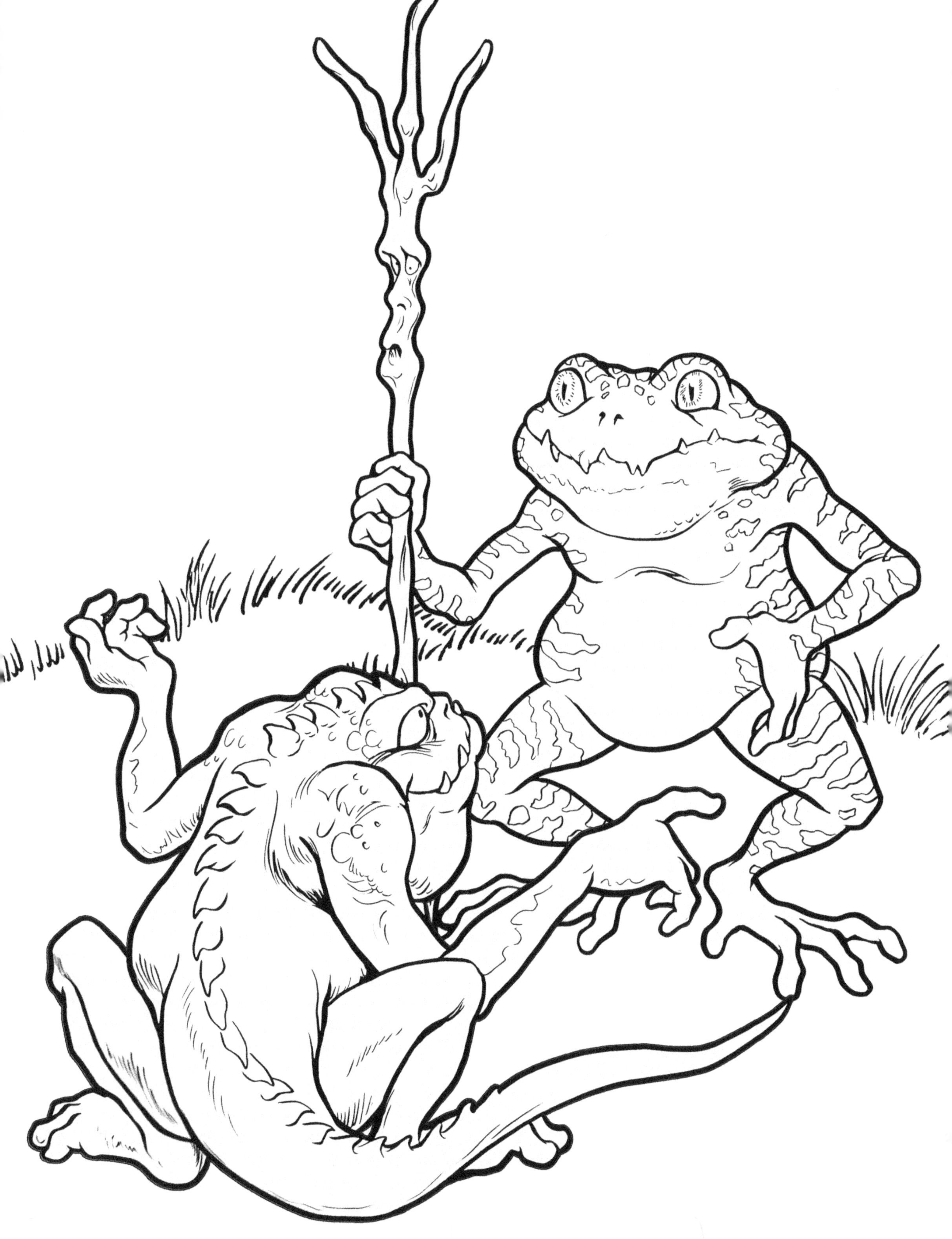

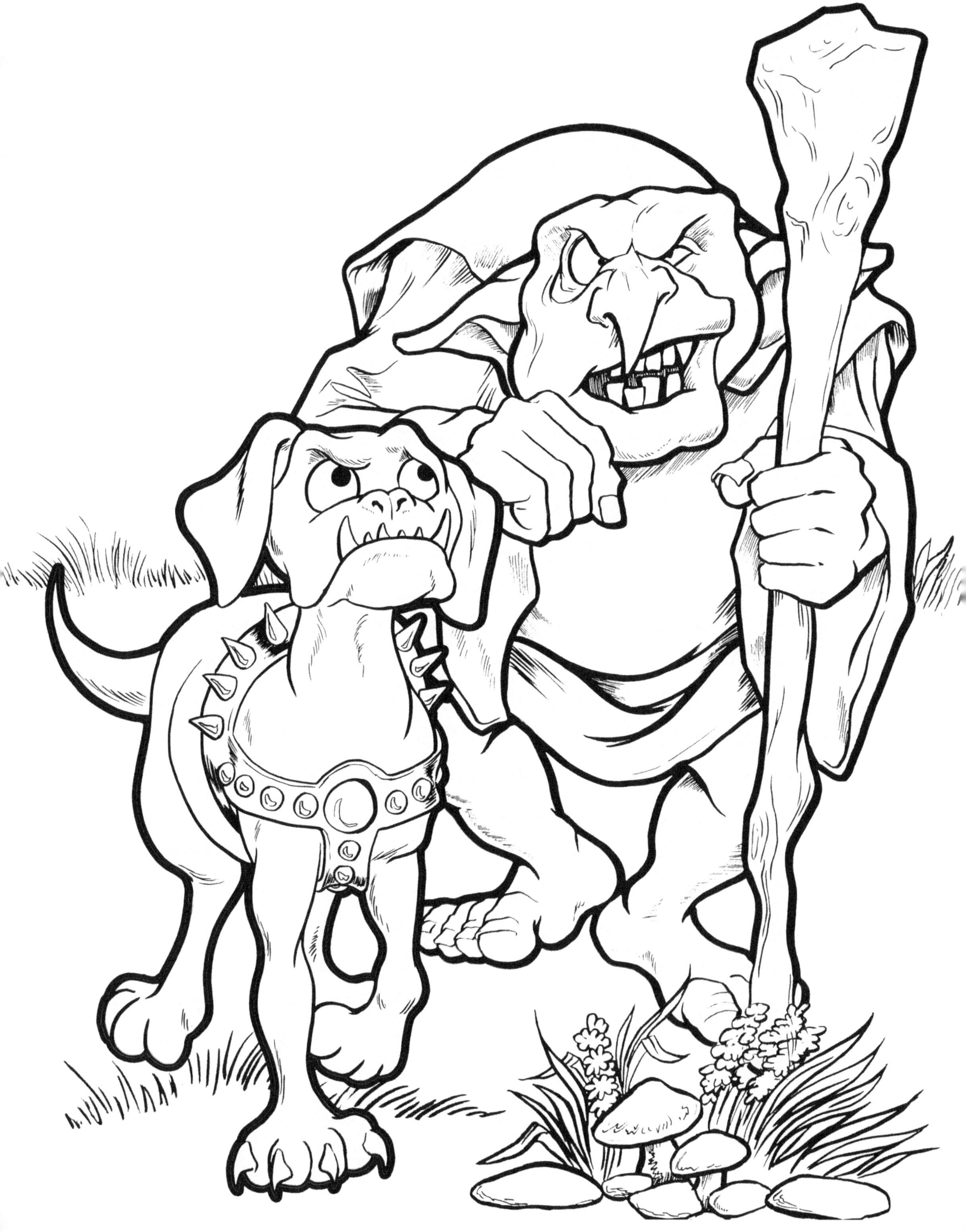

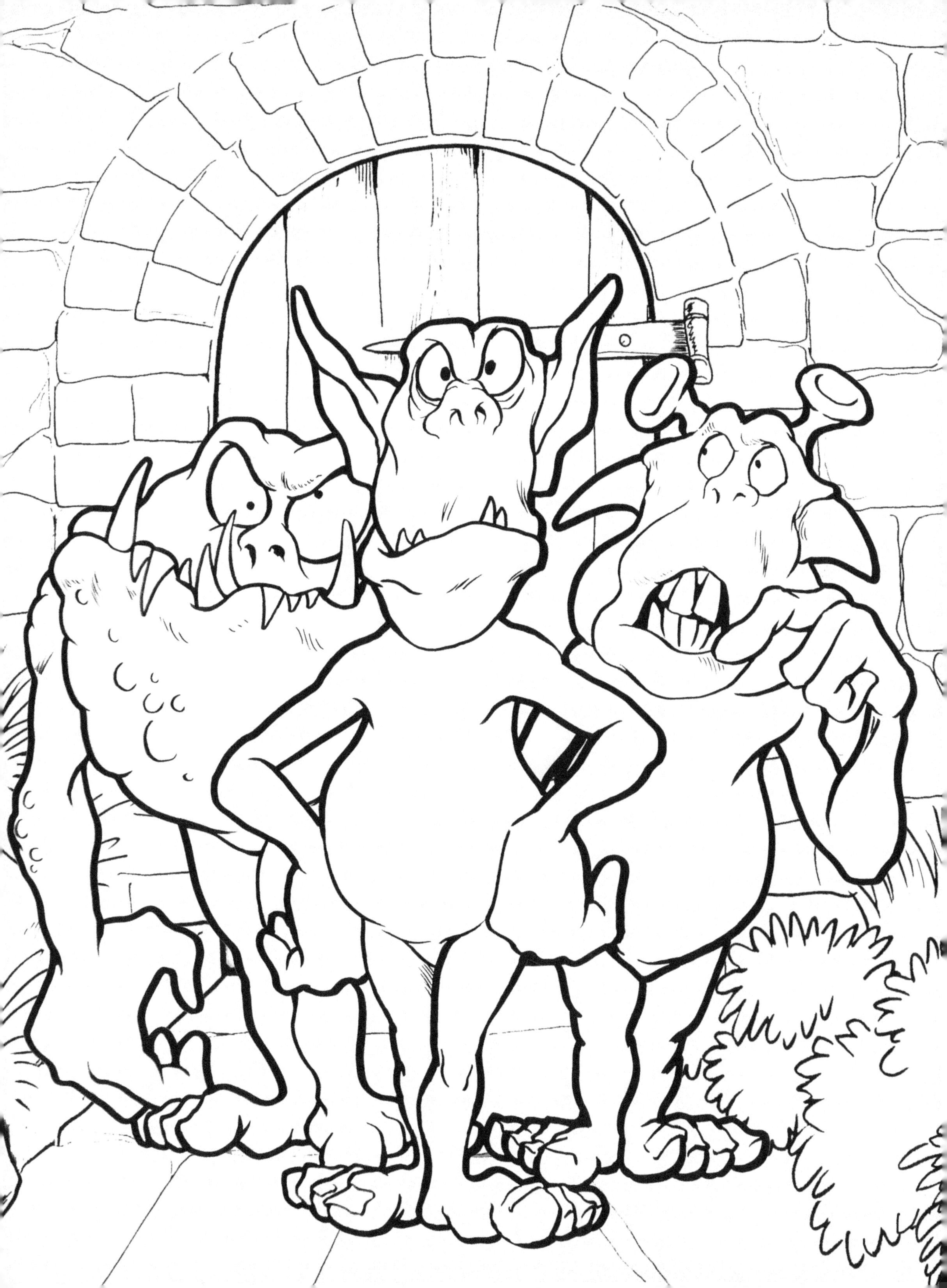

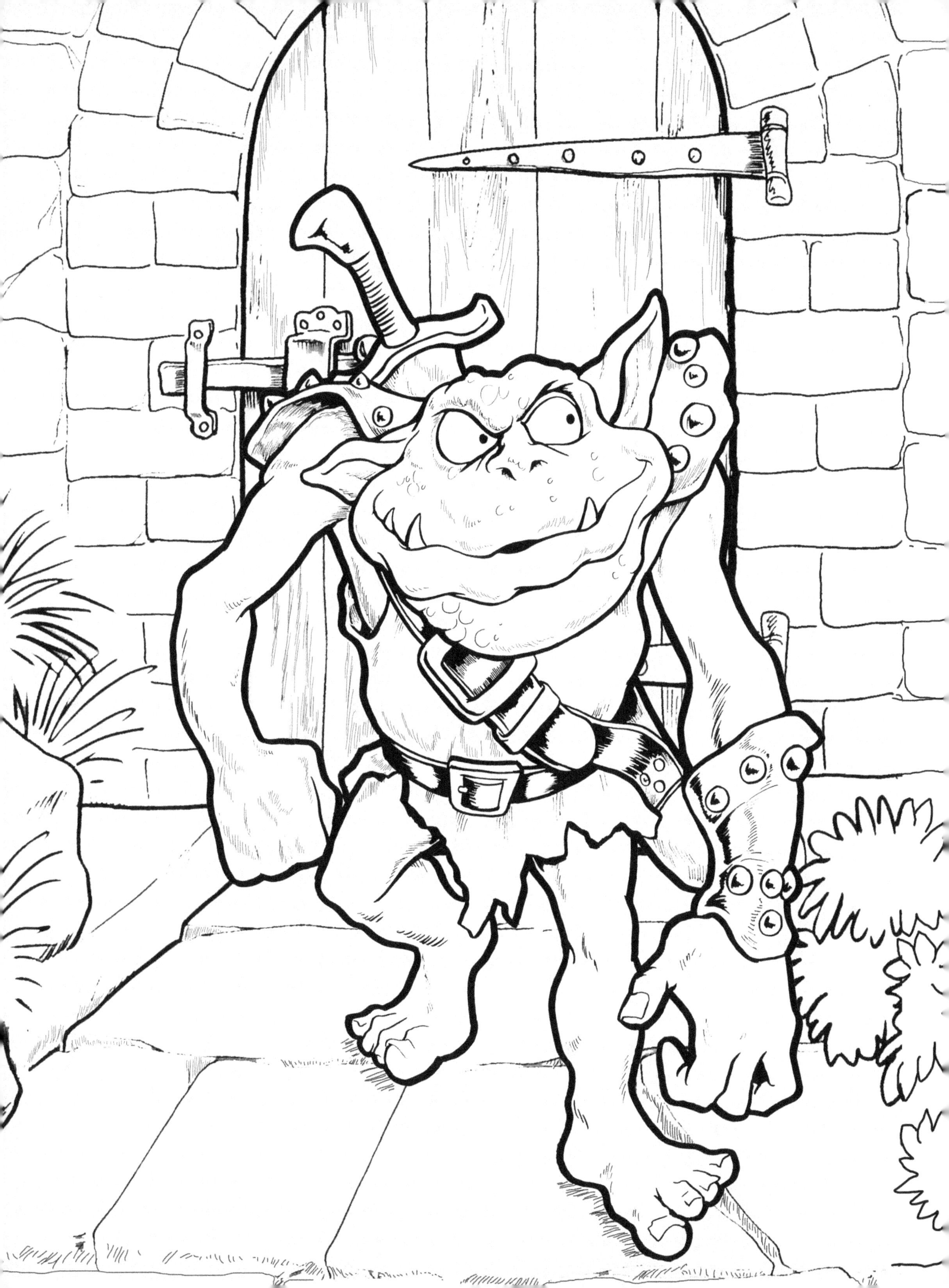

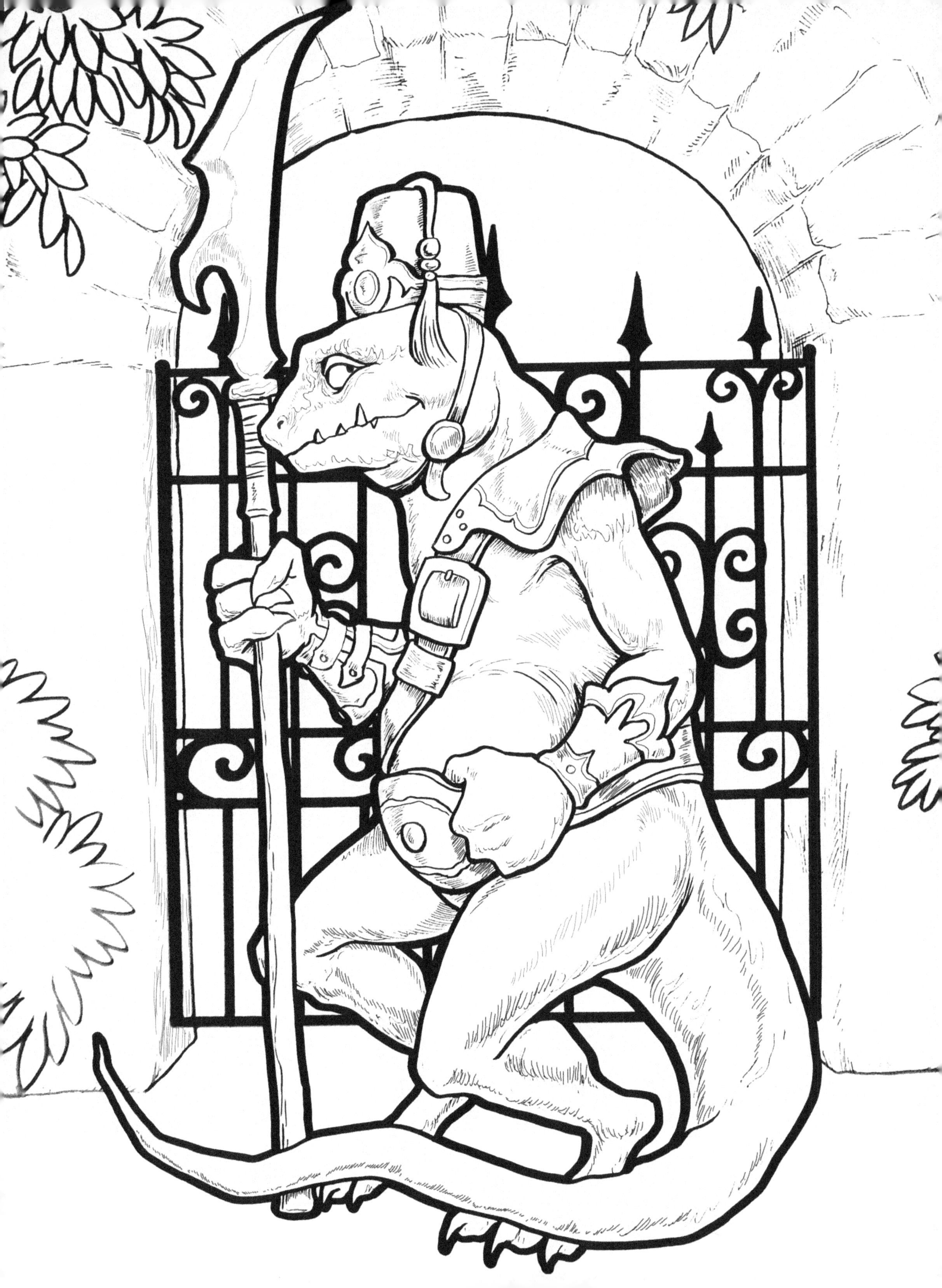

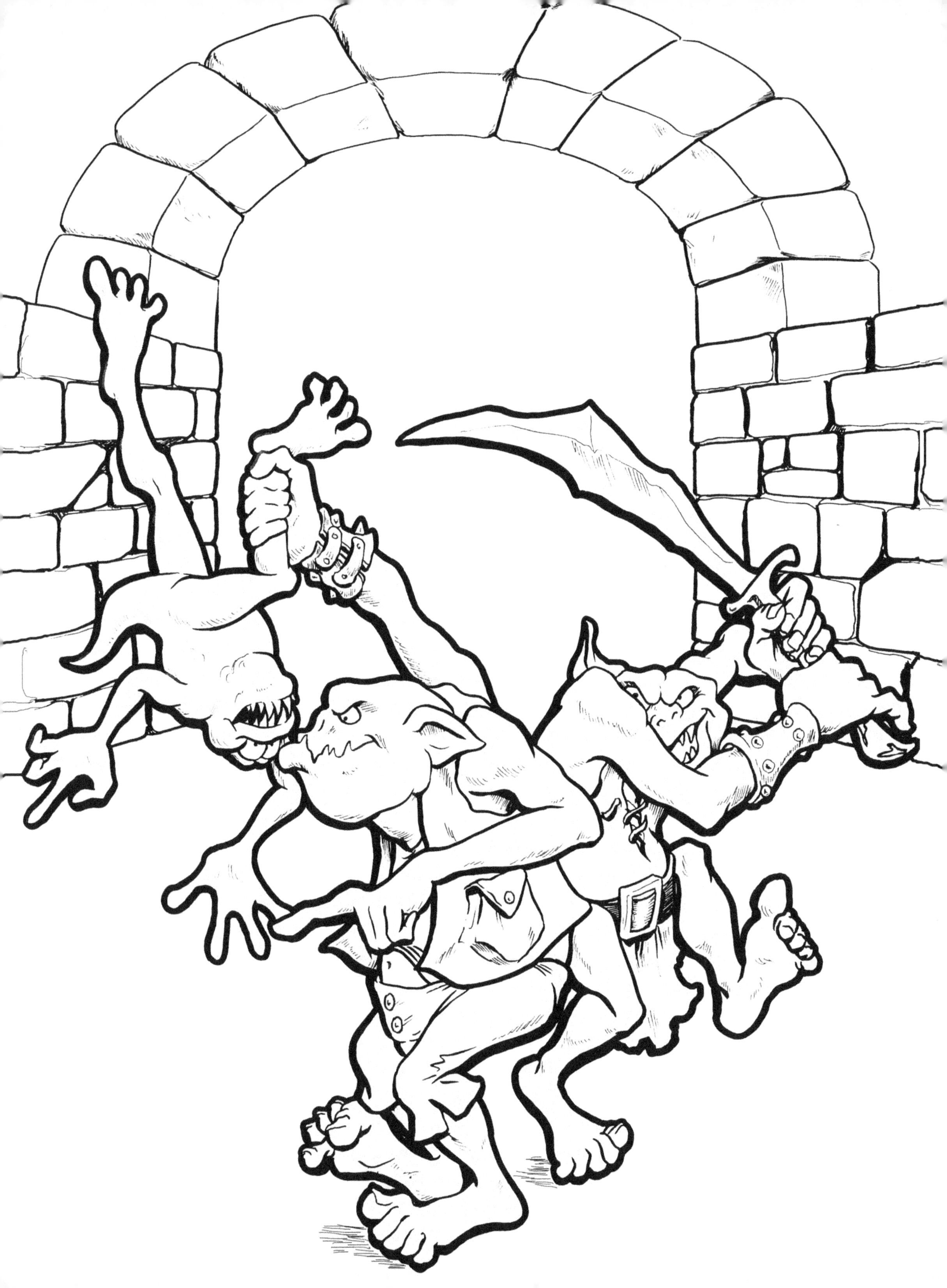

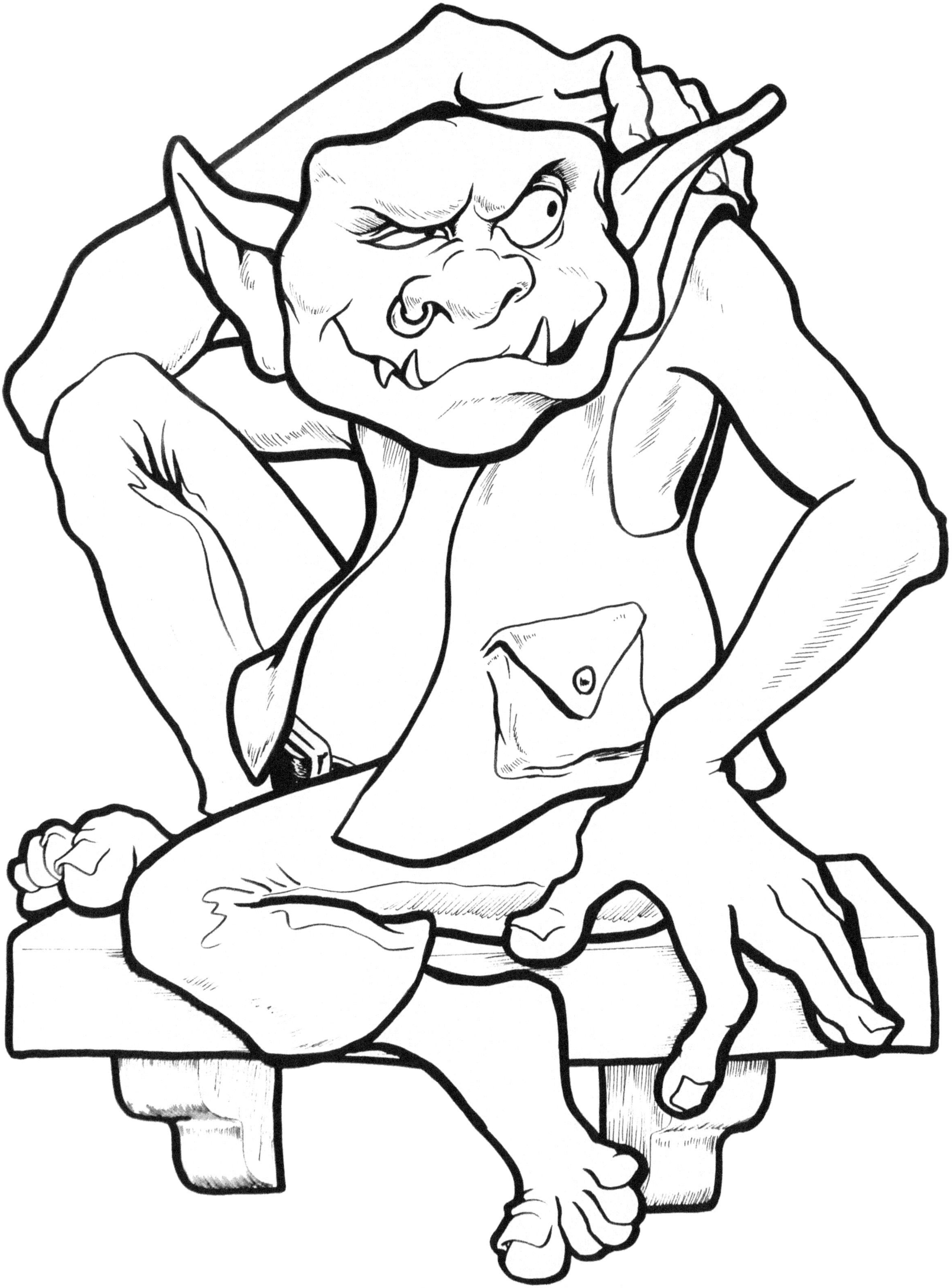

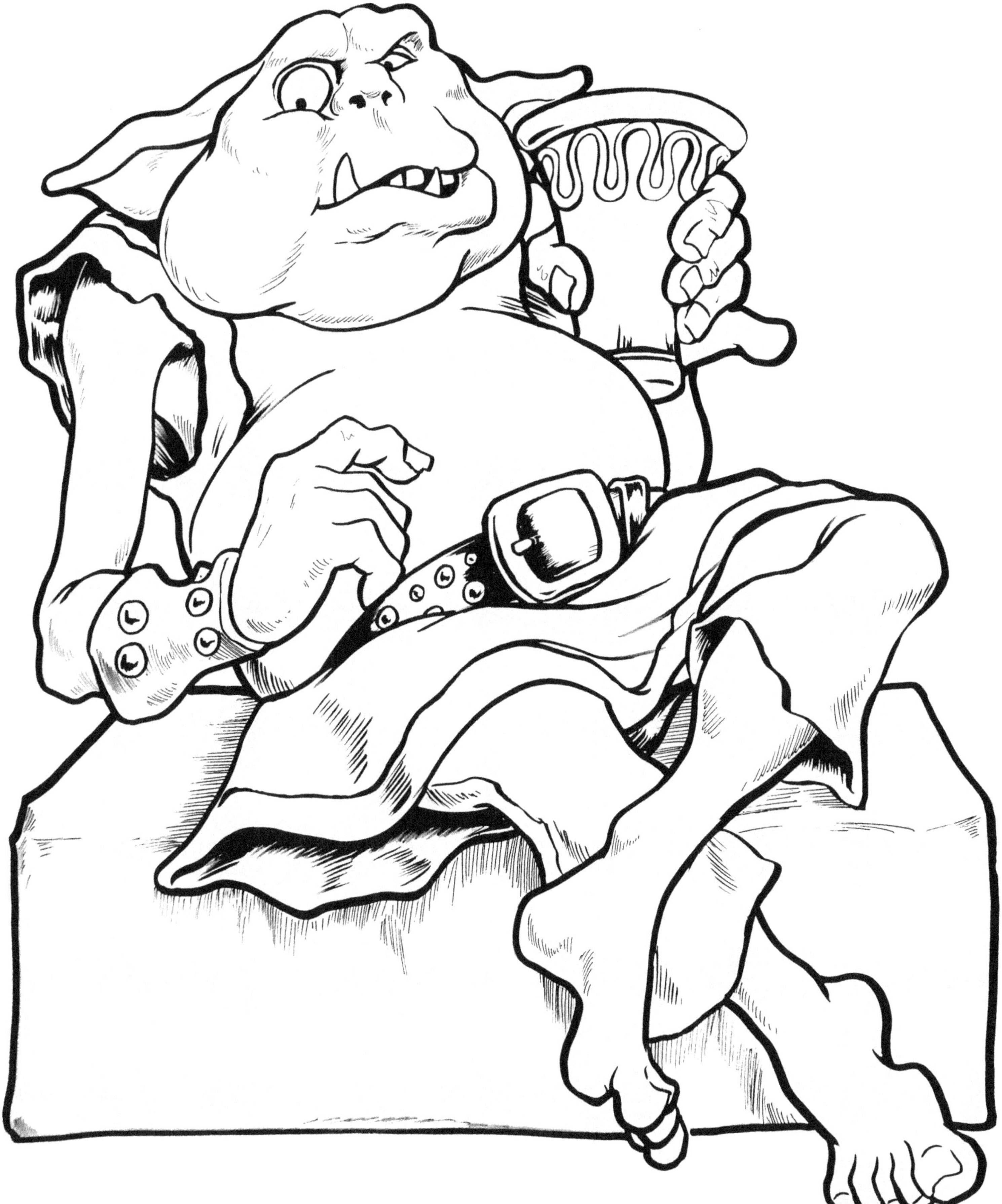

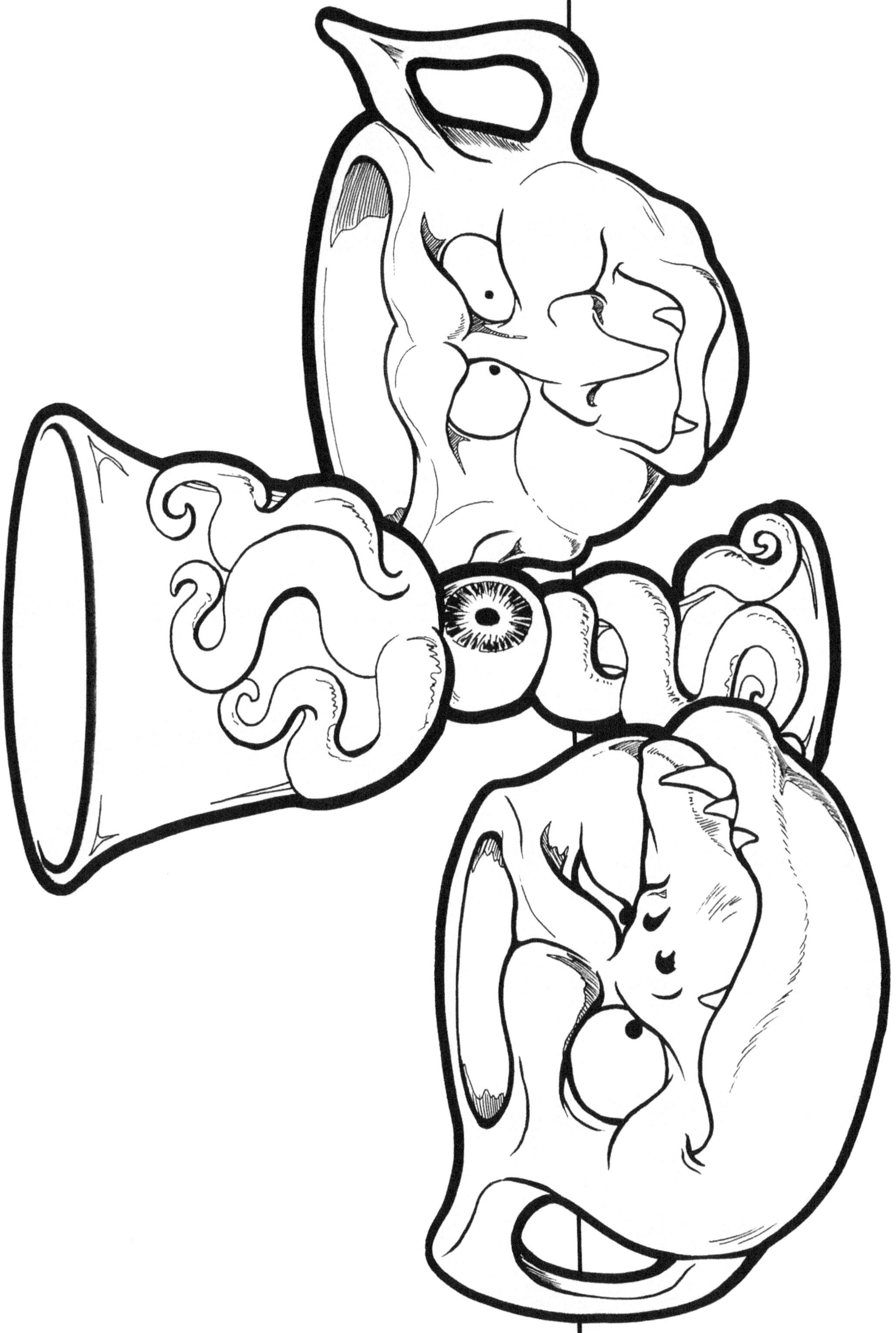

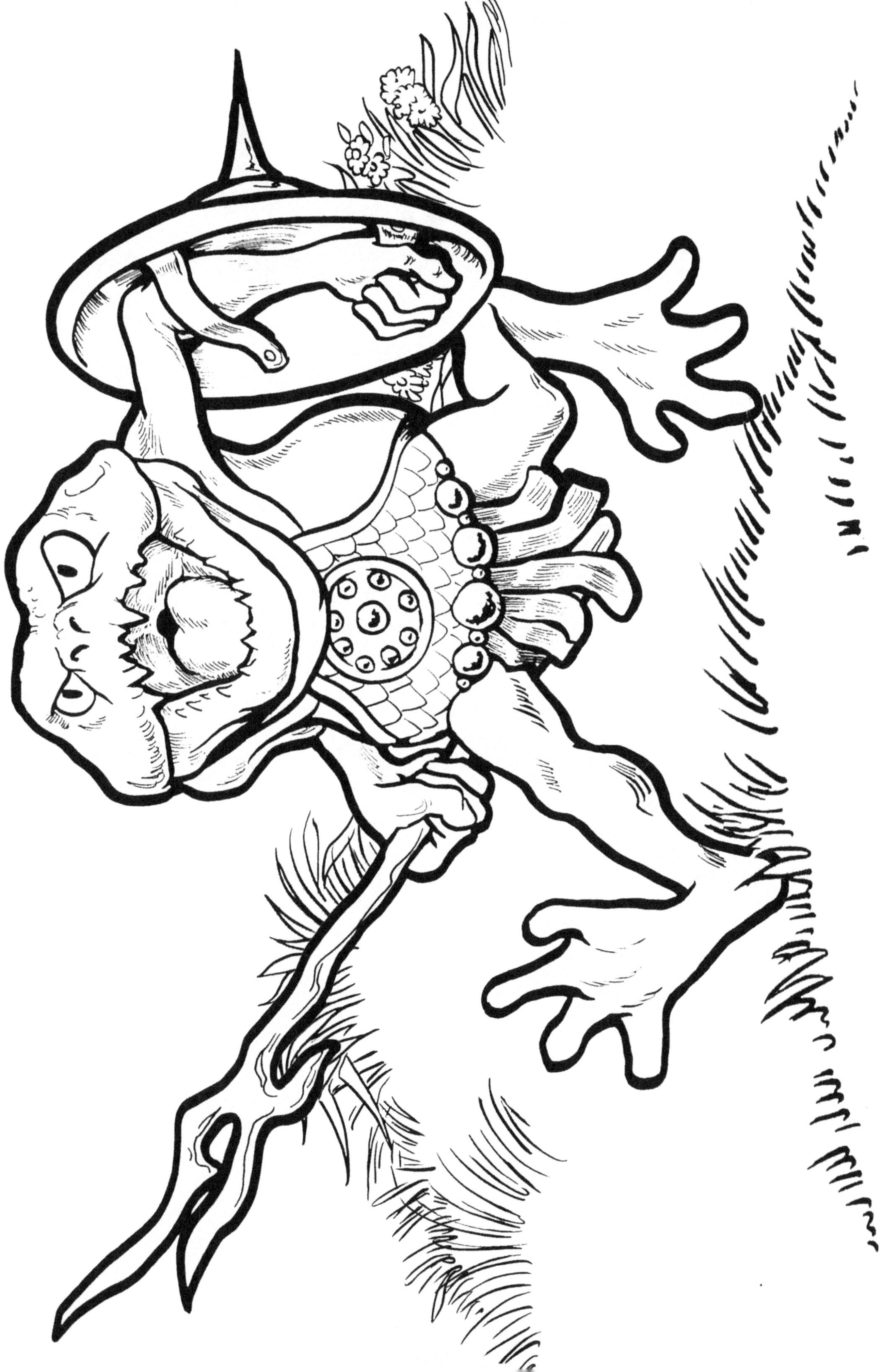

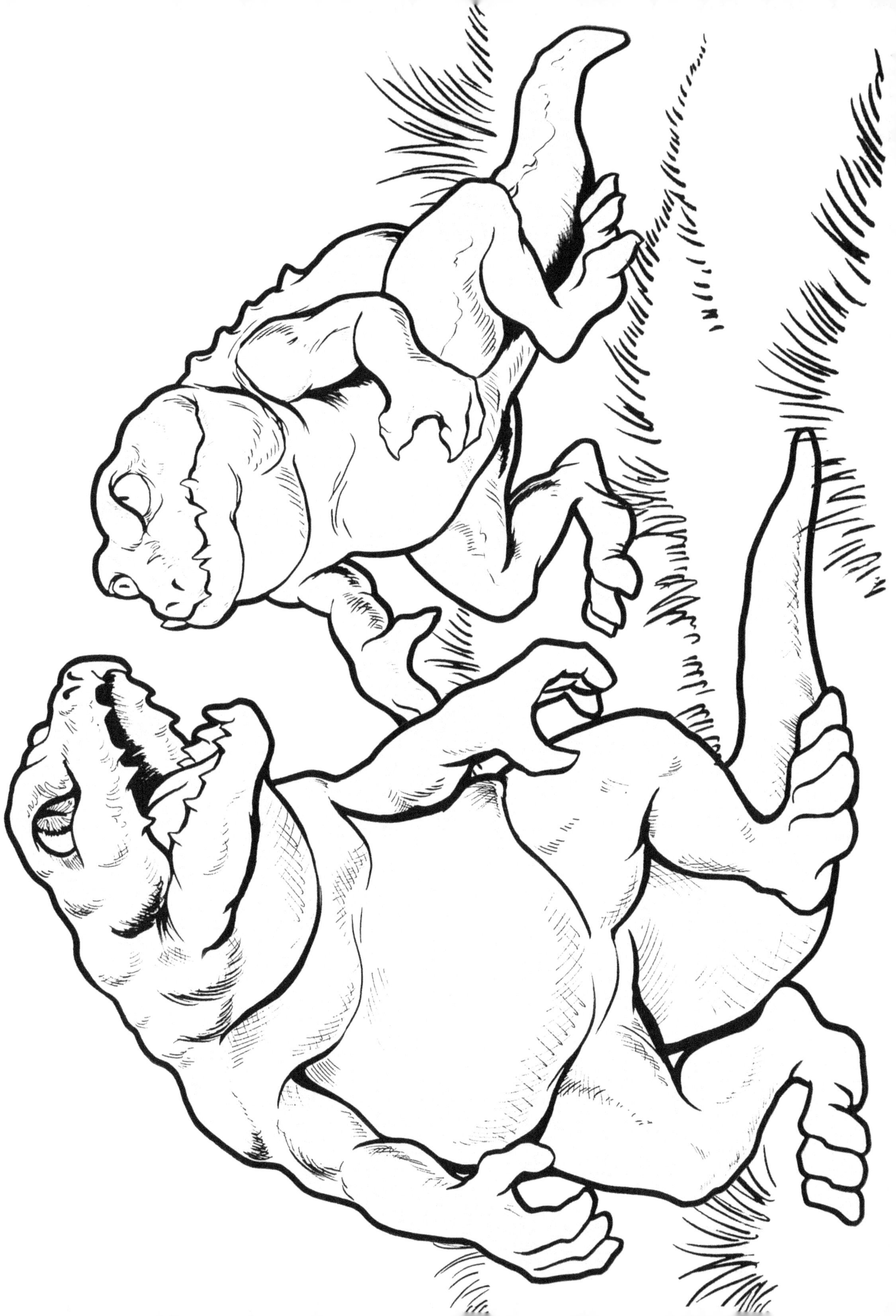

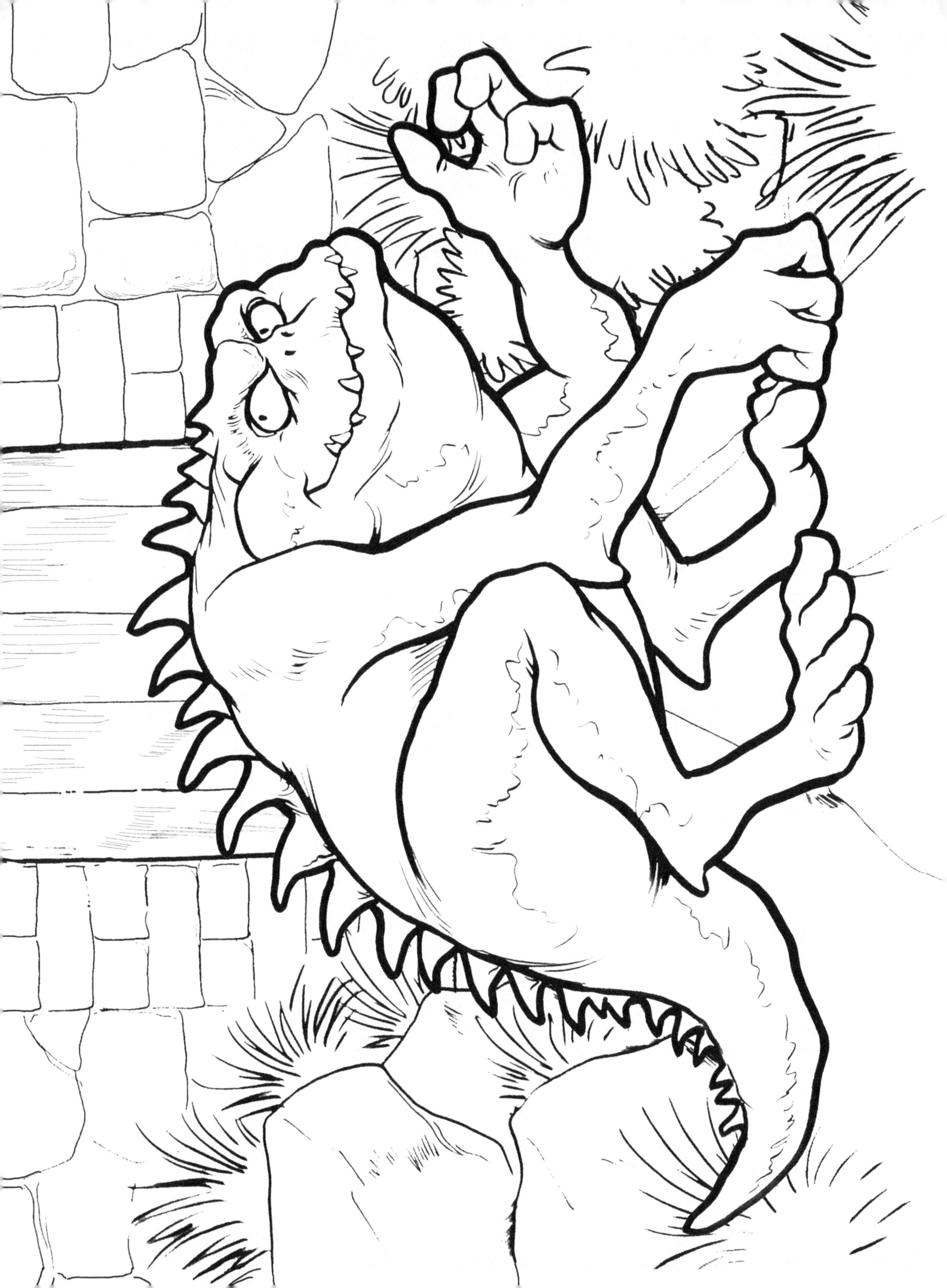

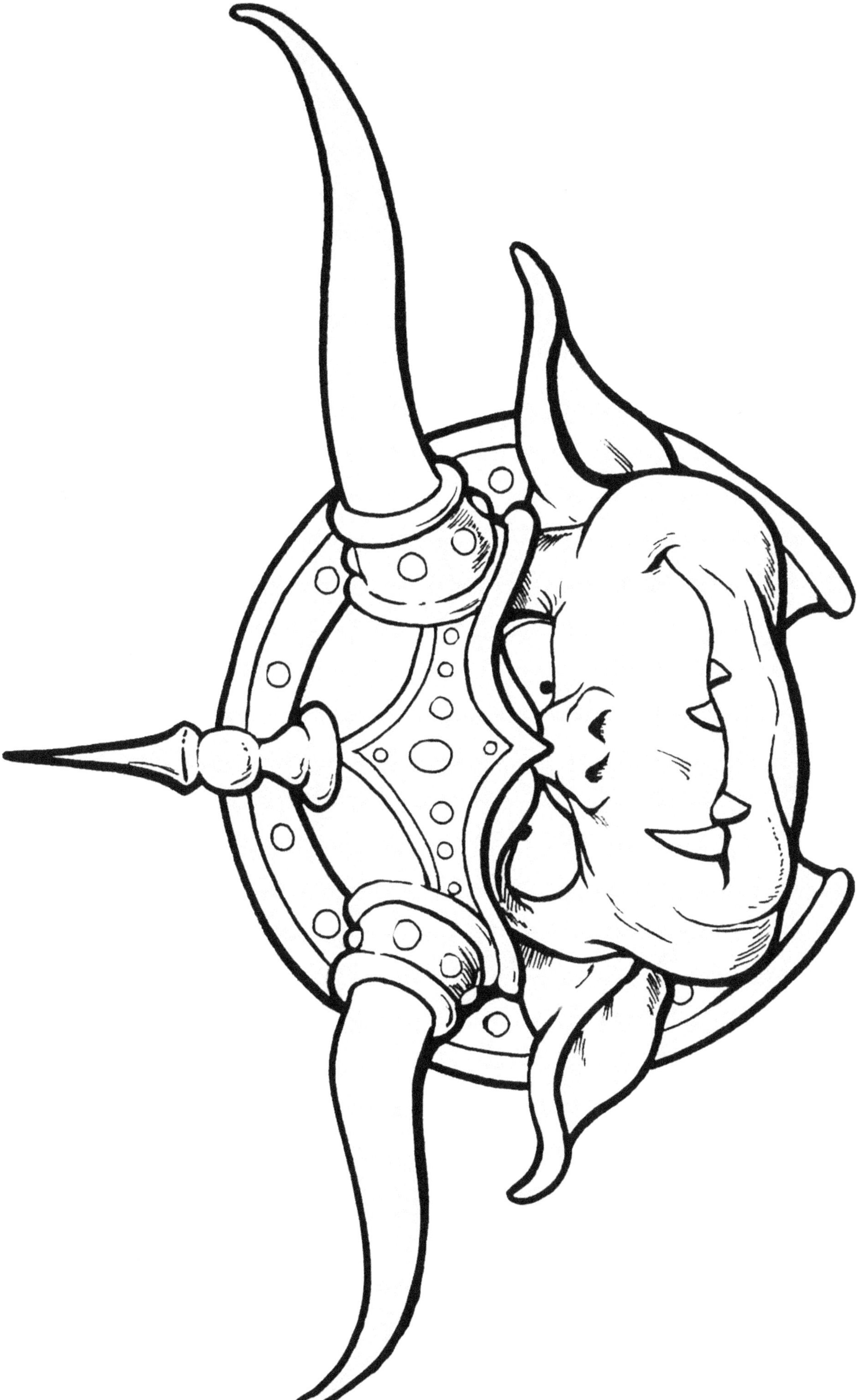

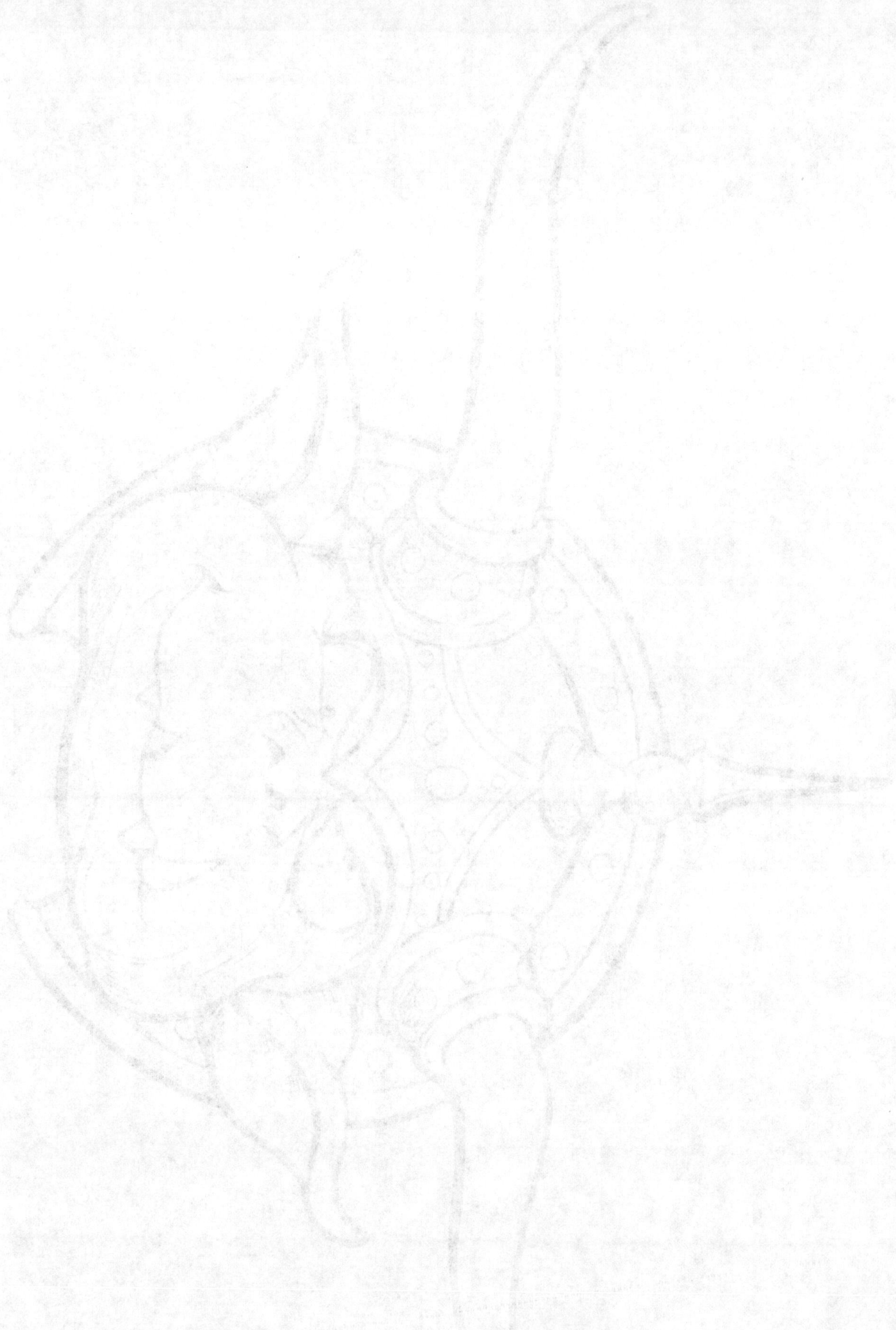

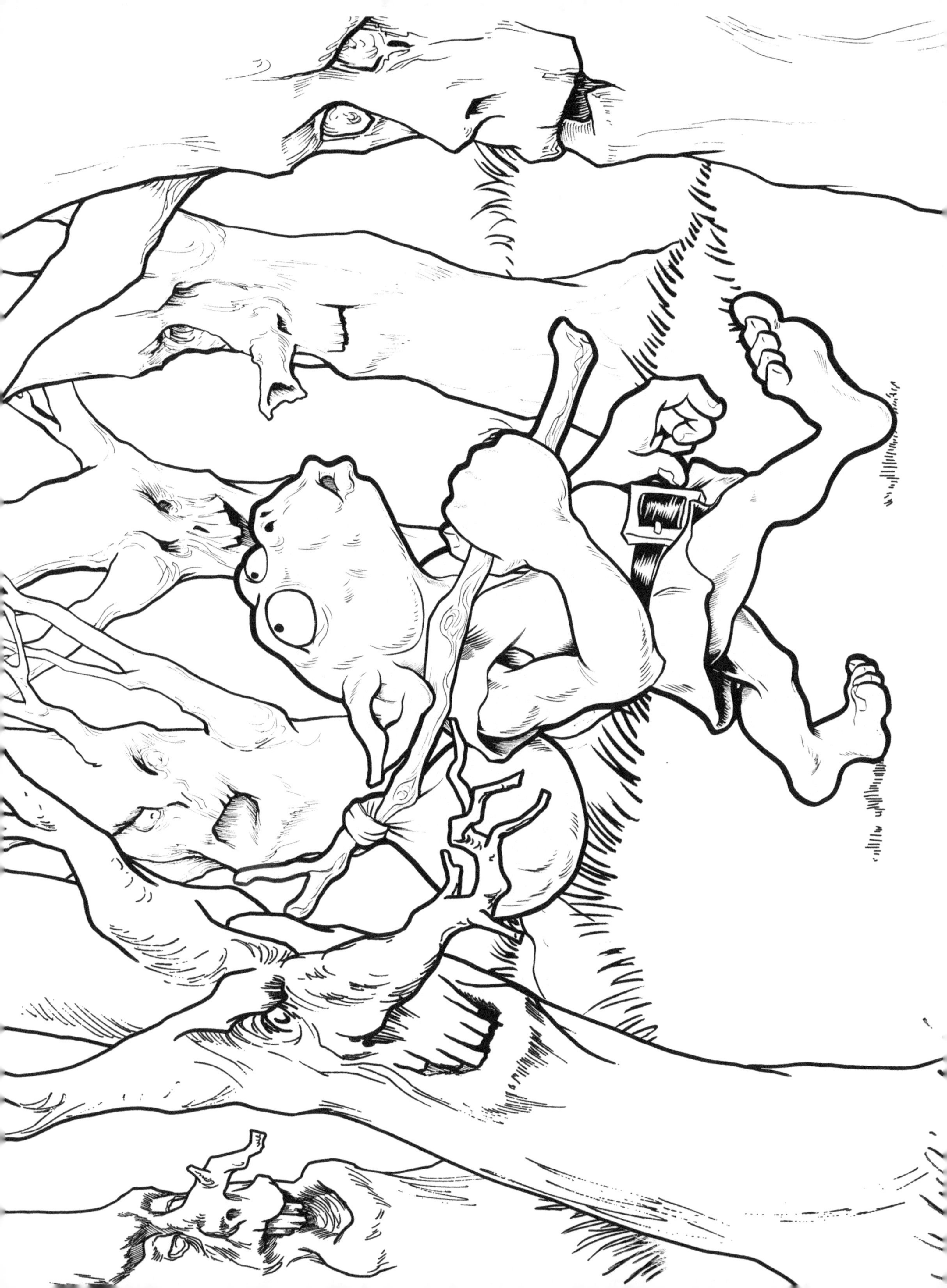

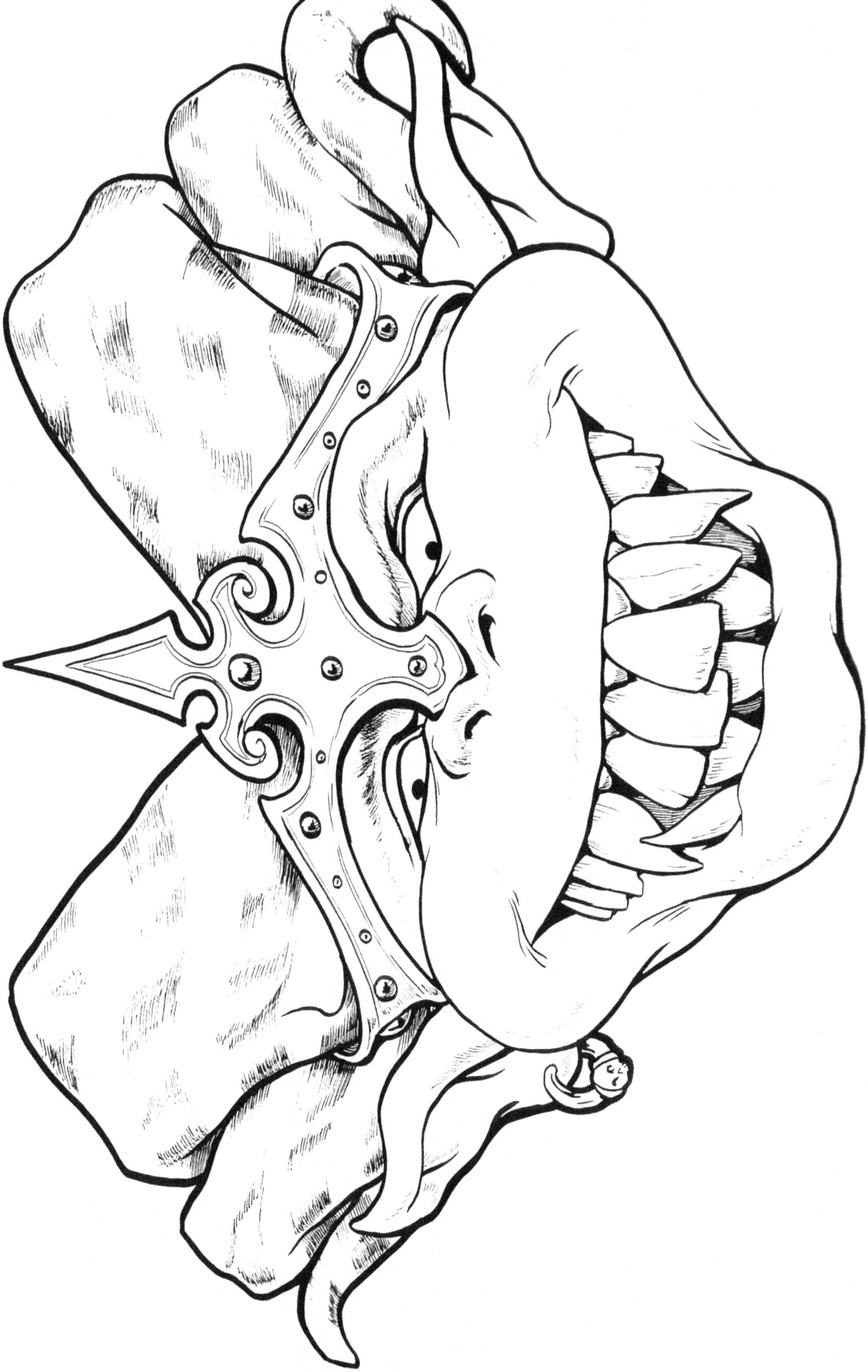

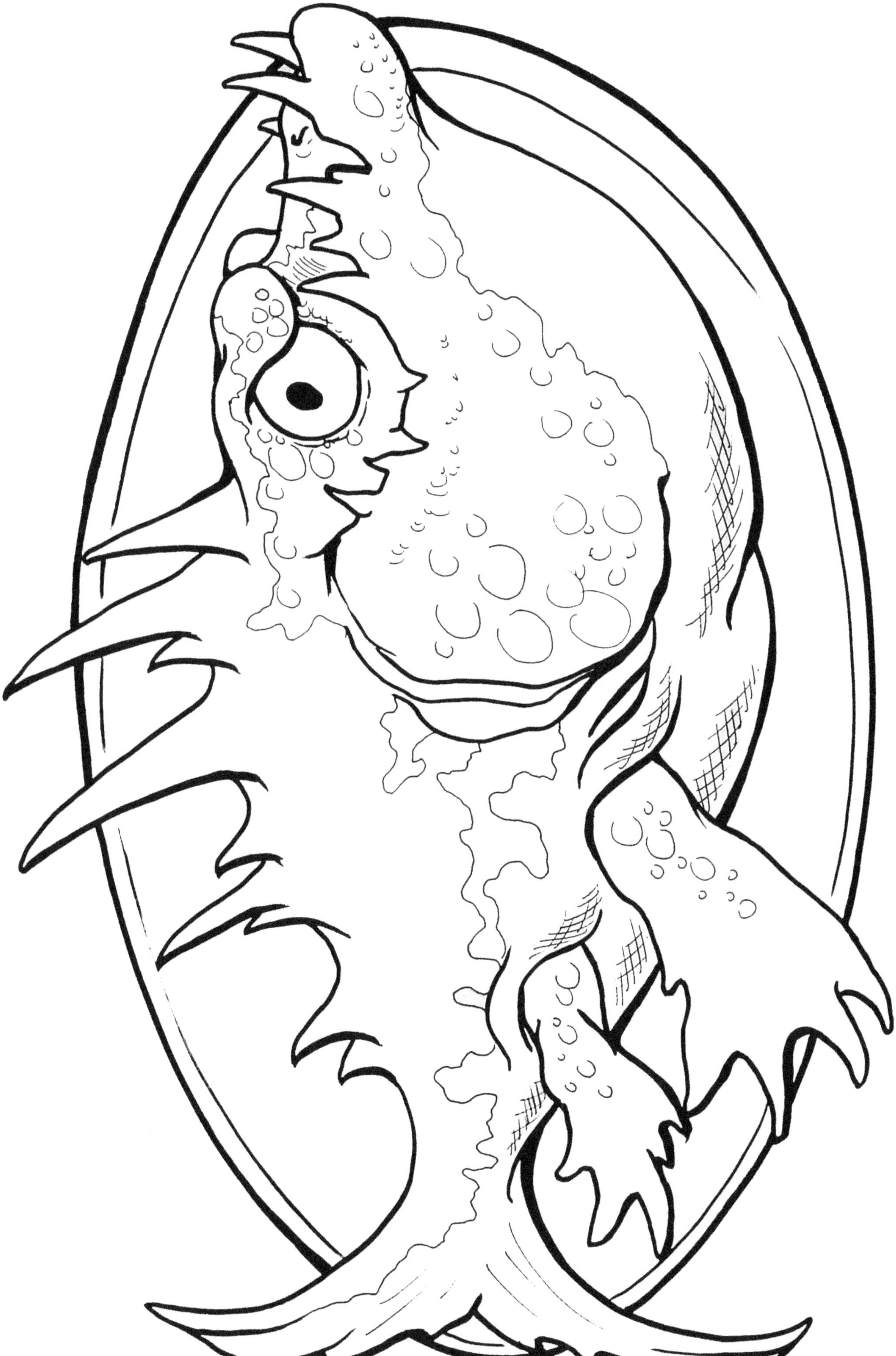

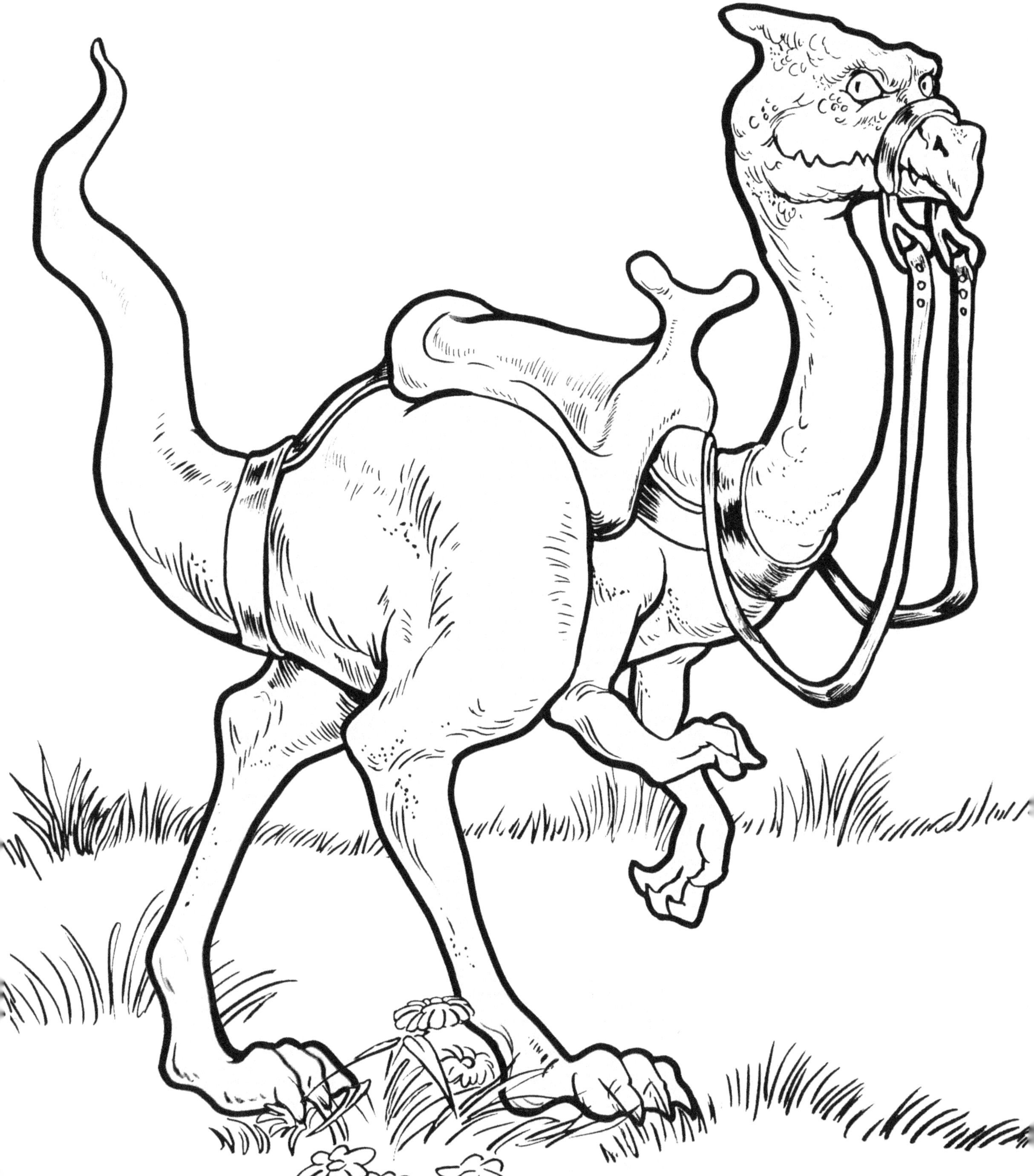

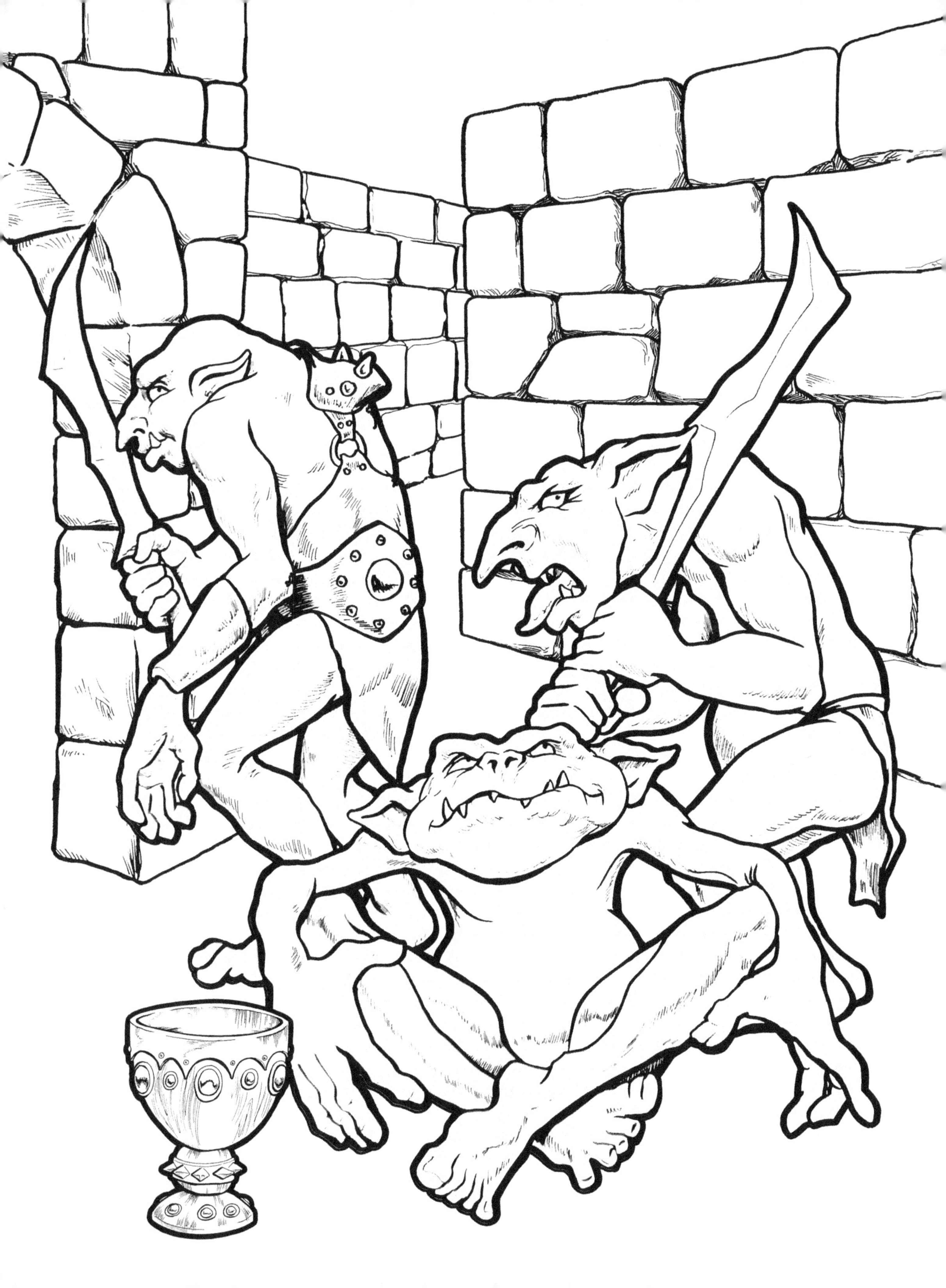

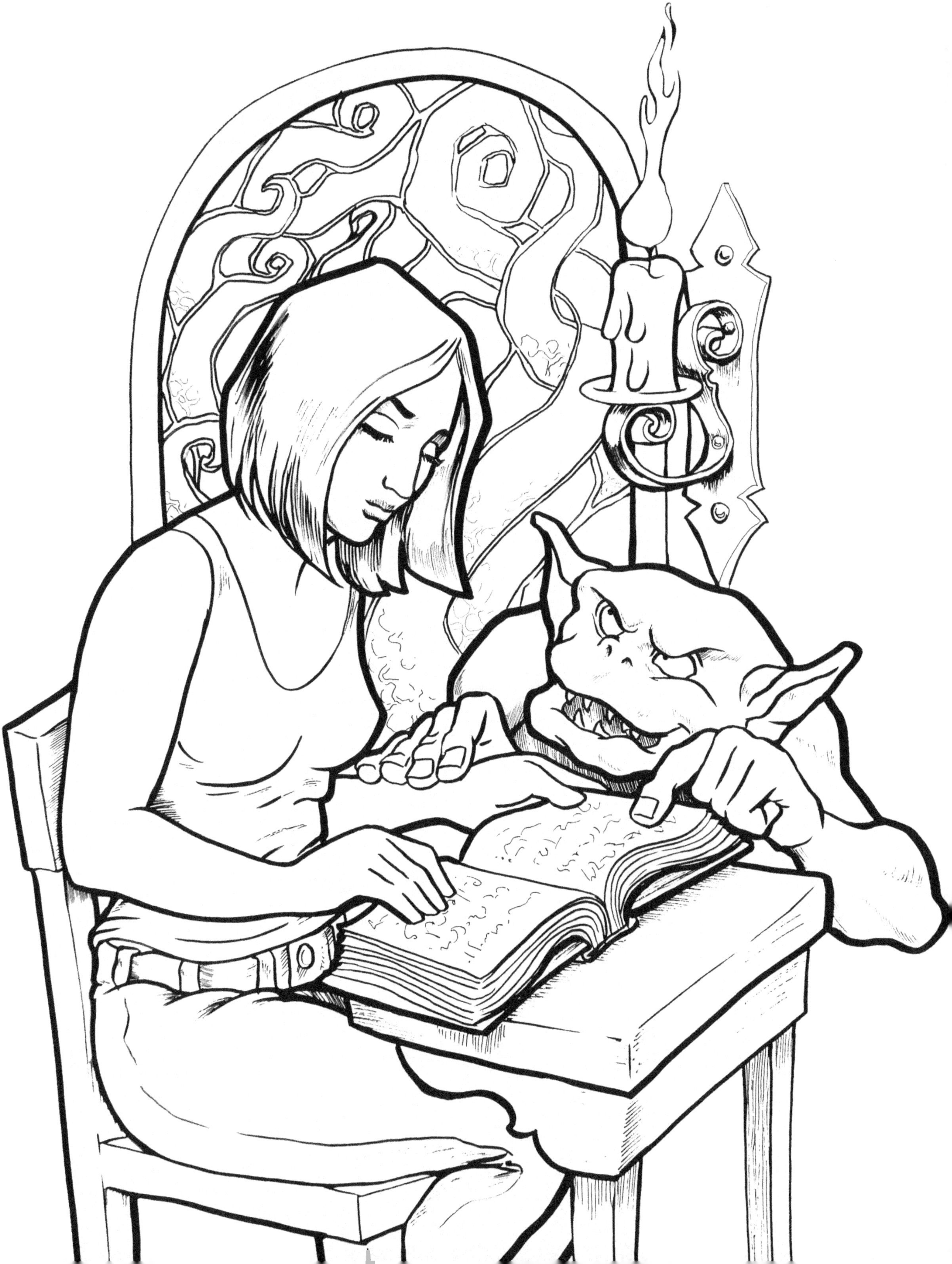

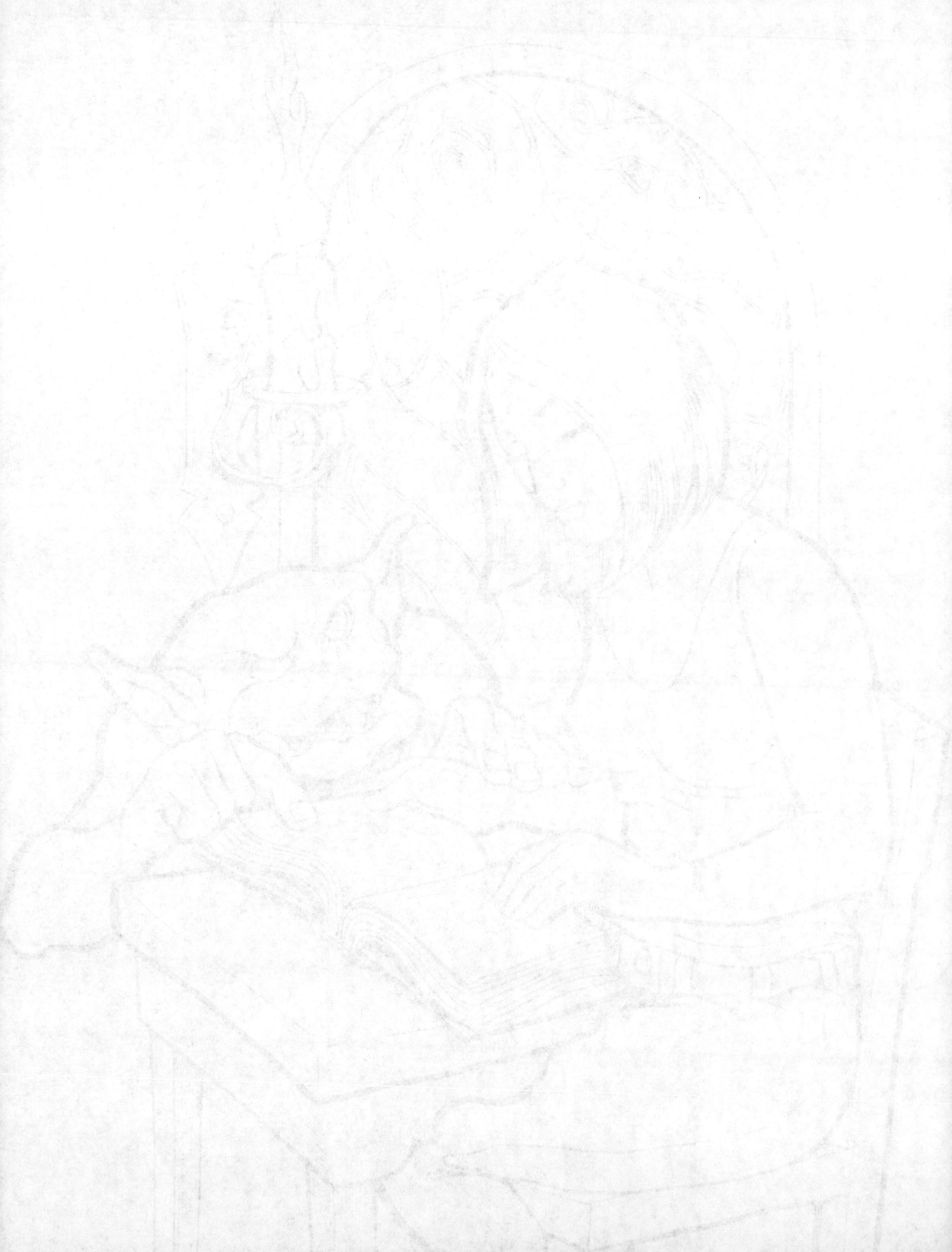

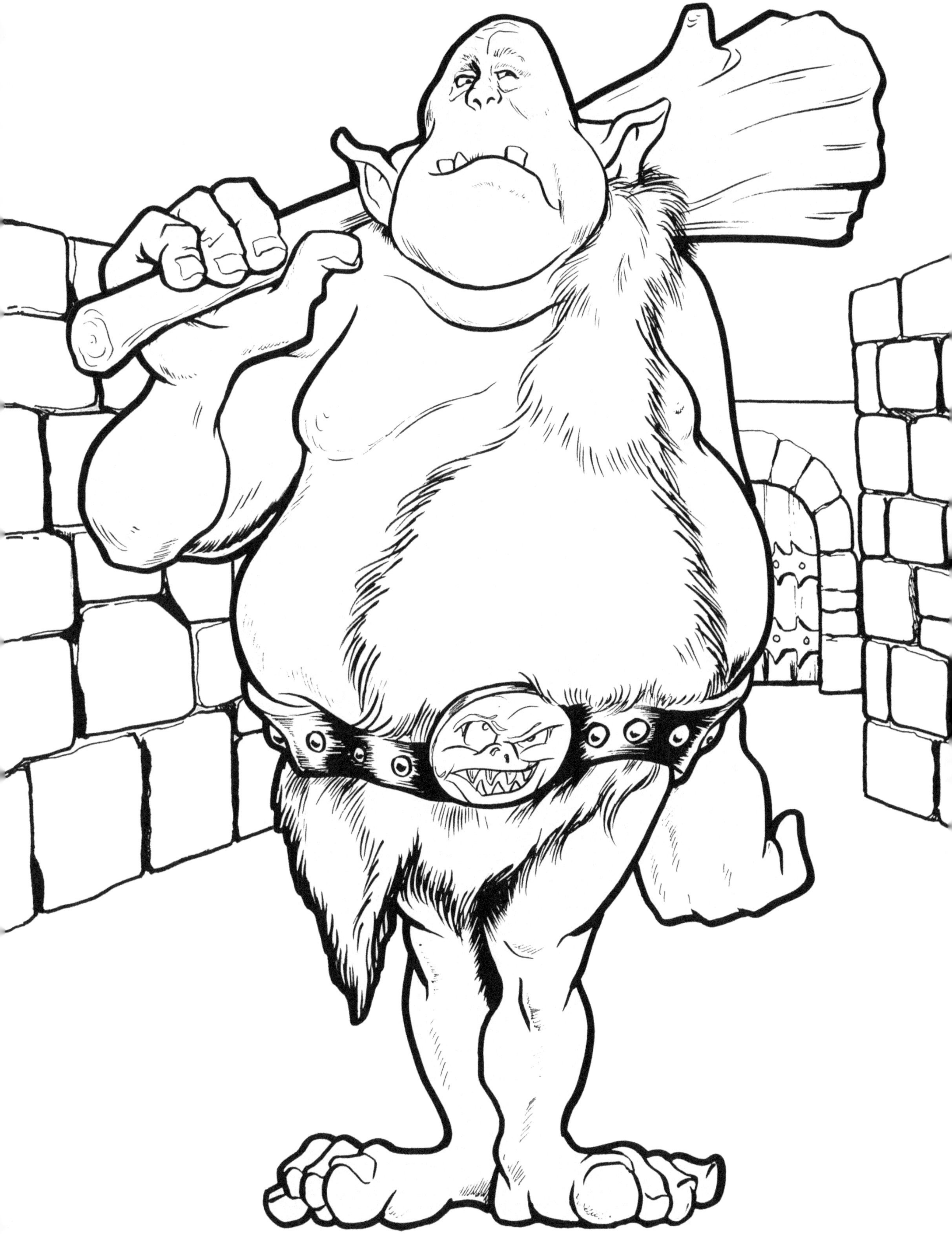

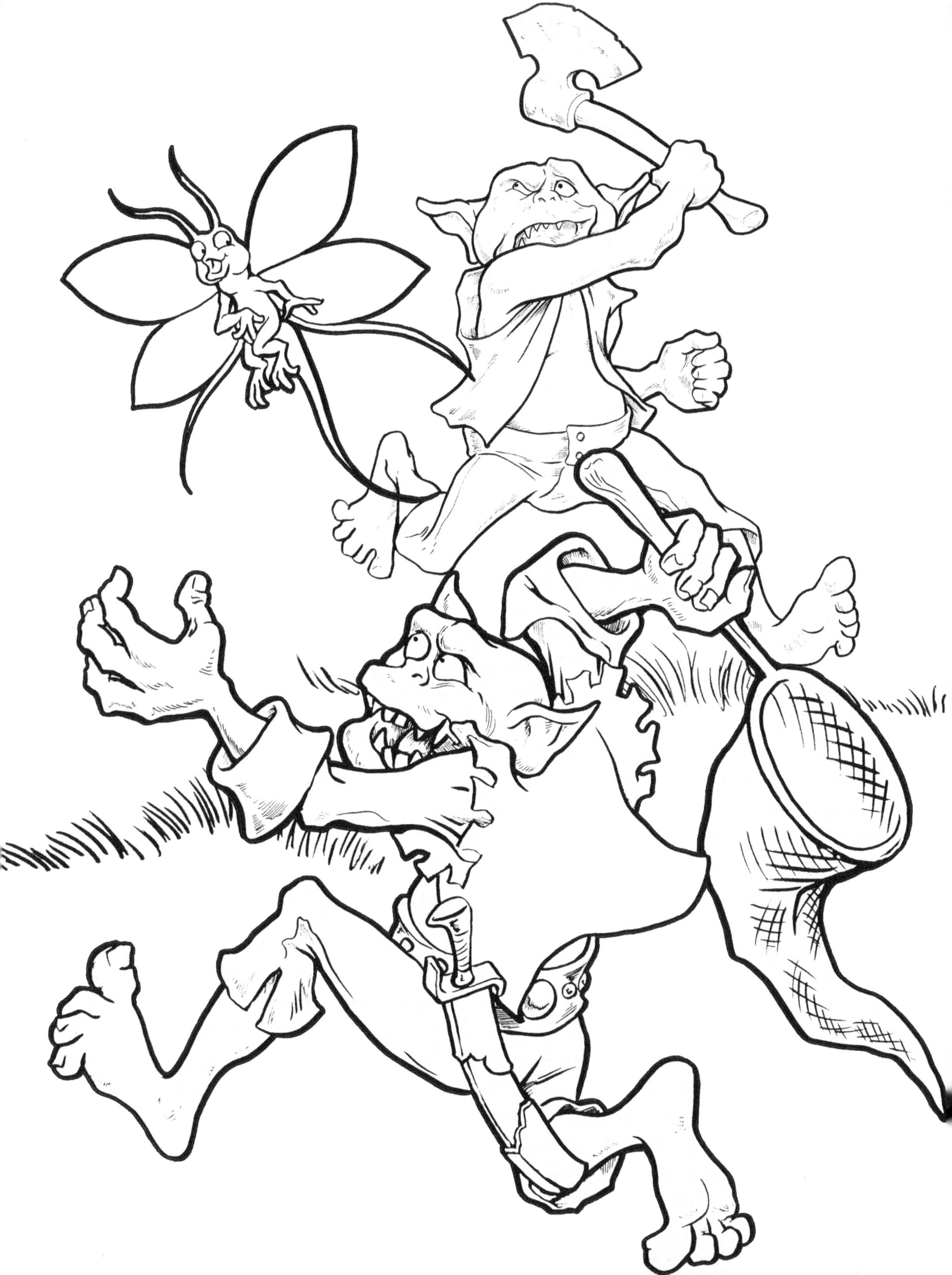

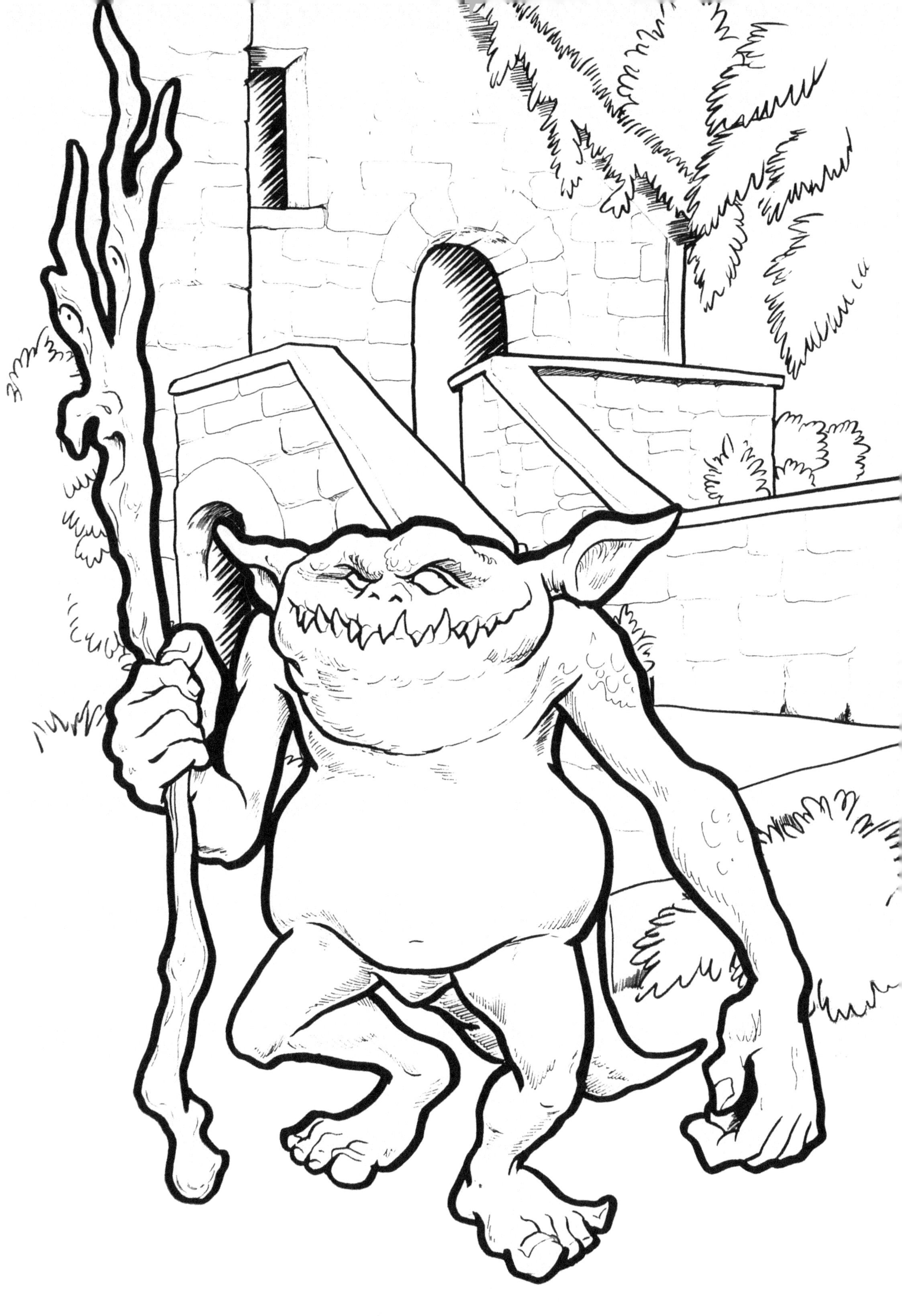

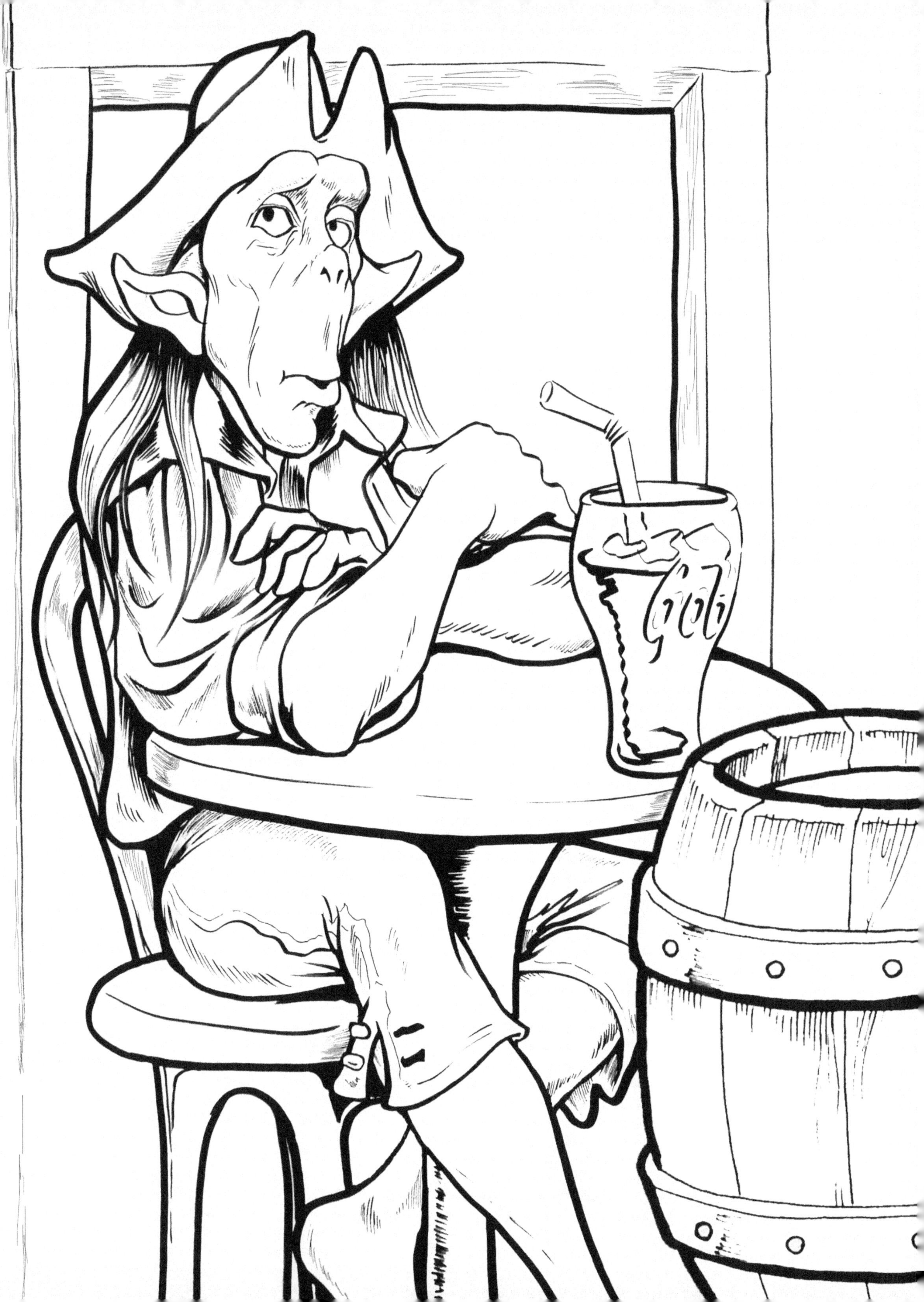
Goli

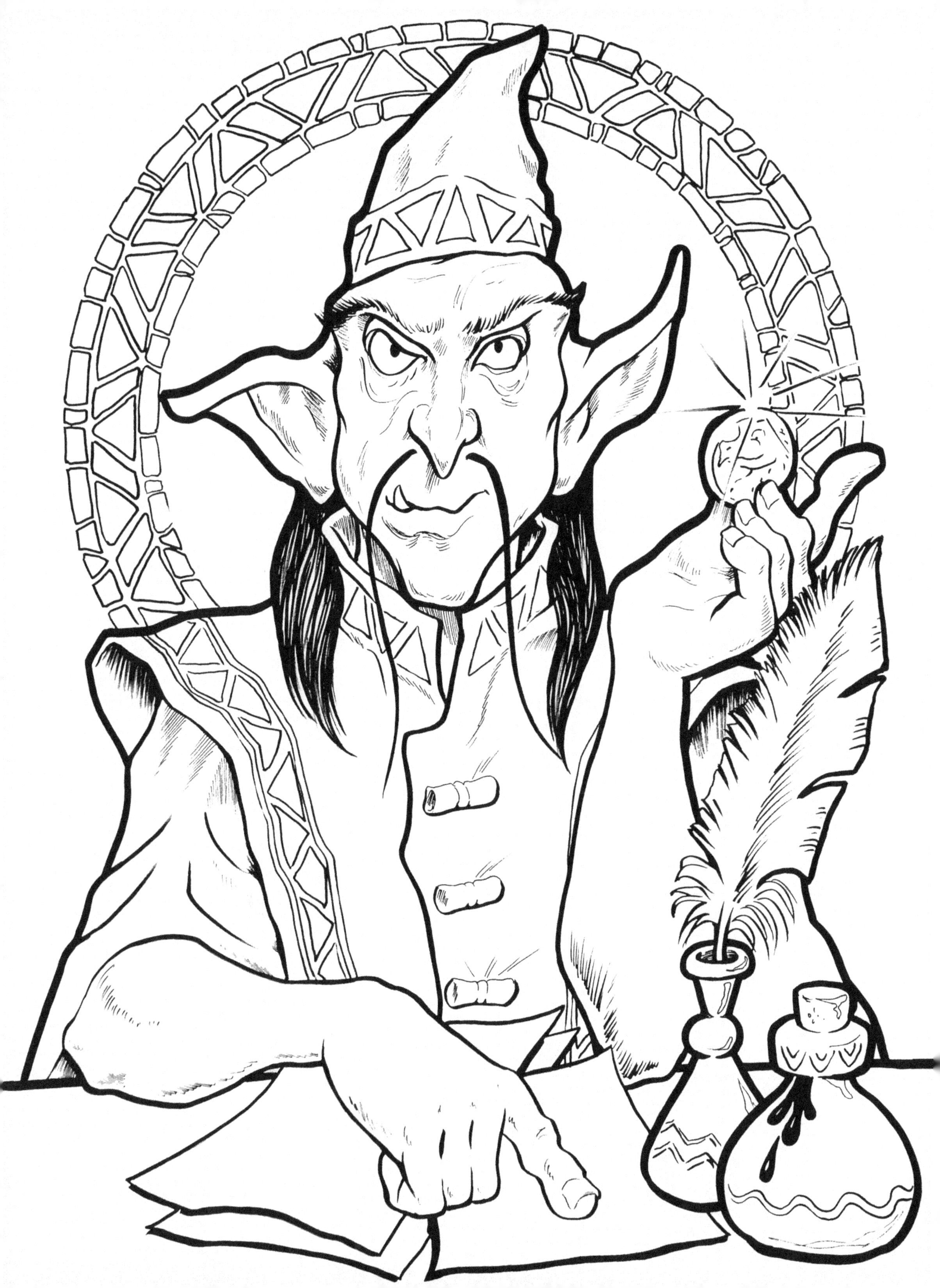

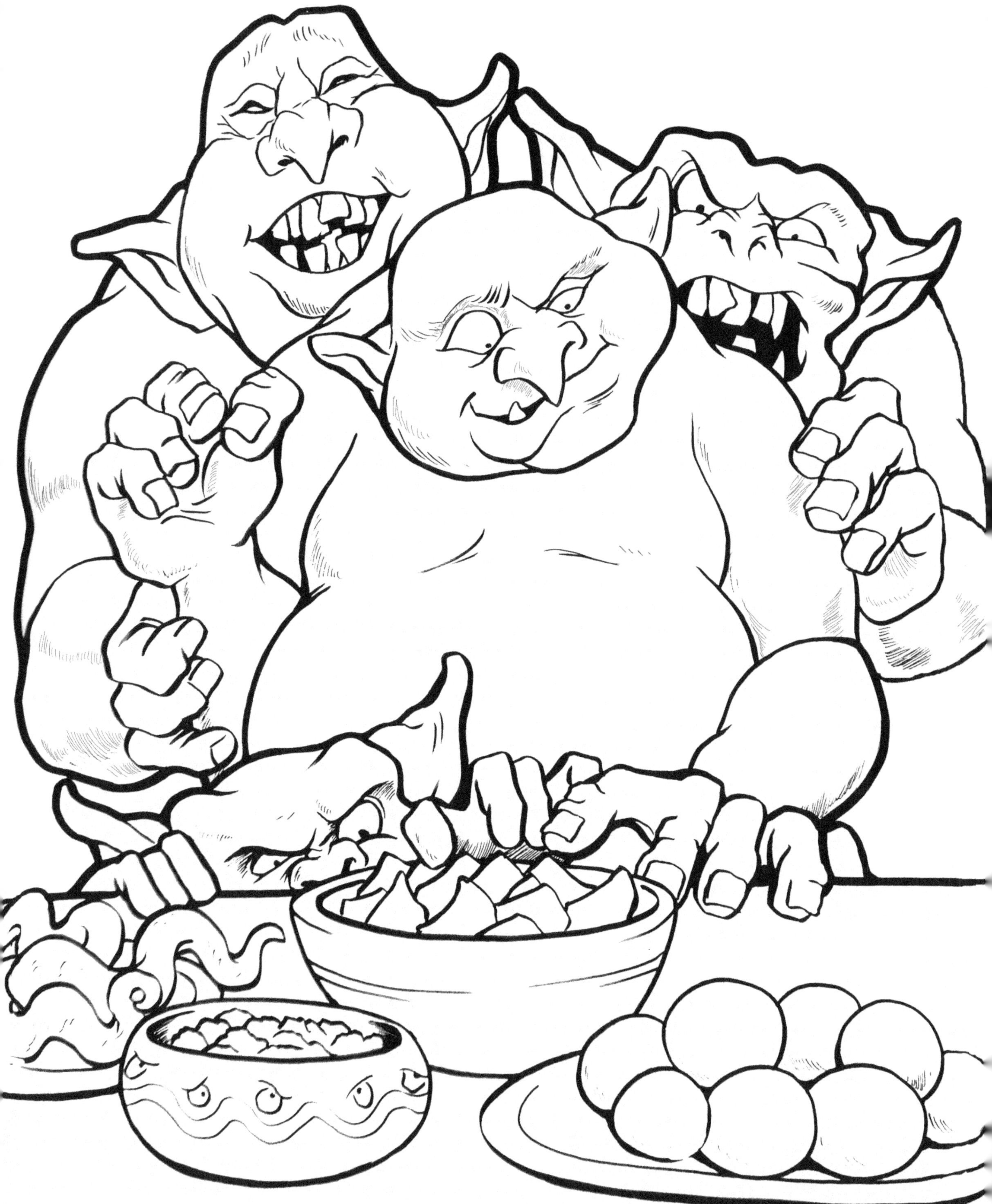

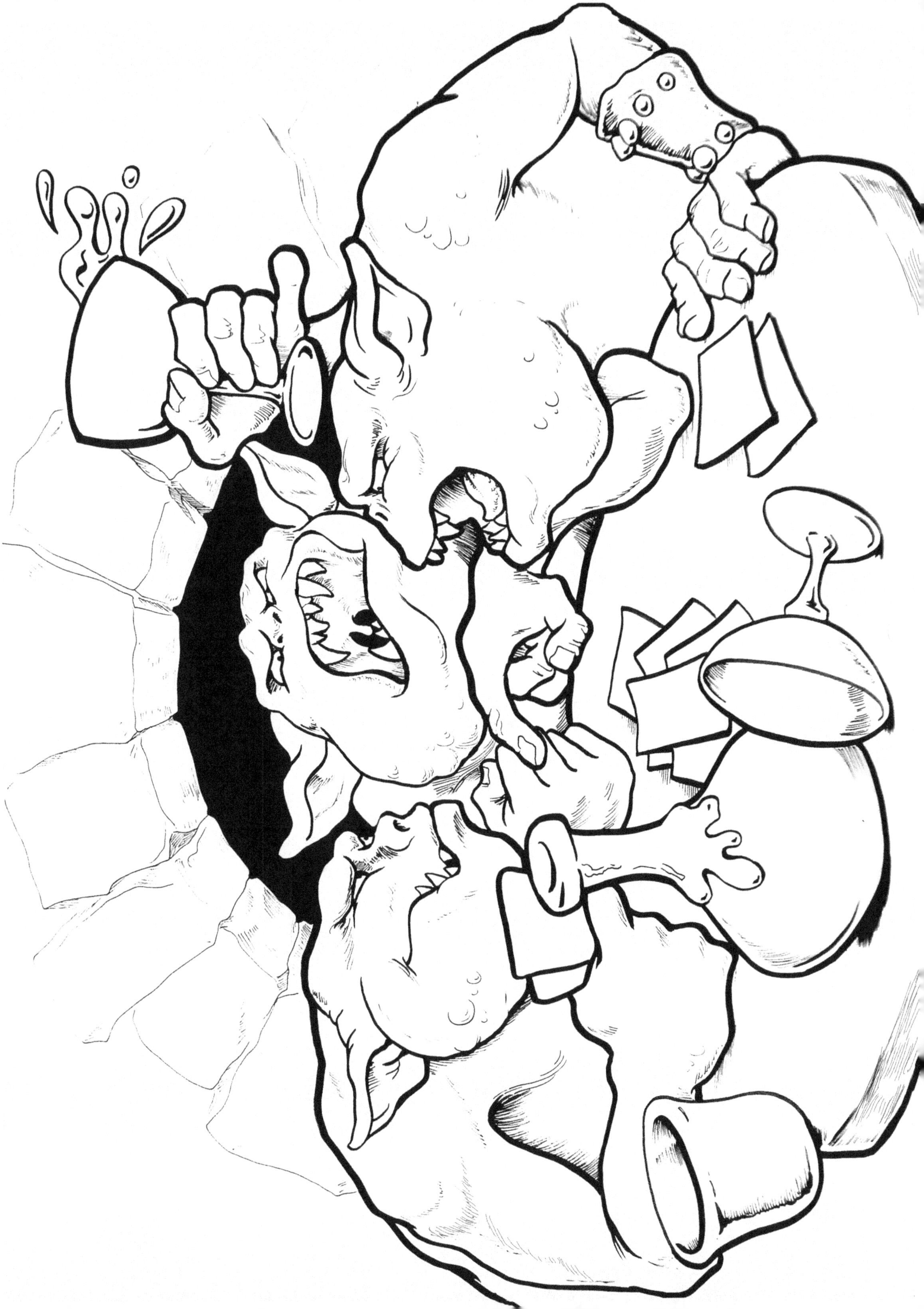

www.ingramcontent.com/pod-product-compliance
Lightning Source LLC
Chambersburg PA
CBHW080612180526
45168CB00007B/2876
* 9 7 8 1 5 1 7 3 2 6 7 1 5 *